In Search of Leadership

Or "Sailing With Roland"

Best wishes !

Jm K

By J.M. Kelly

1

"Leadership is based on inspiration, not domination; on cooperation, not intimidation."

-William Arthur Wood

Table of Contents

Dedication

There are many people to recognize when covering a concept as broad and profound as leadership. Along the way, so many contribute to your growth as a leader with support, encouragement, or outright advice. This book is dedicated to the following:

- To Margaret Kelly, the matriarch of our clan, who not only gave me a life, but also showed me how to live.

- To Bronwen, Peter, Alex, and Brianna, the lights at the end of every tunnel.

- To my teachers, for pointing the way: John Crews, Tim Kempson, Mary Saraco, Bob Reid, and Jim Bagli.

- To the teachers and staff of Lafayette School, who taught me what it really means to be a leader.

- To Gene Hastings, the quintessential school principal, and to the wonderful superintendents with whom I've had the pleasure to work: Dr. Carol Conger, Joe Schneider, and Jim O'Neill.

- And, most especially of course, to Roland Barth, for his writings and thoughts, his friendship, and for opening his seaworthy sanctuary to a die-hard landlubber.

Foreword by Roland Barth

Two of my abiding life's passions have been education and sailing. Where they intersect is an even more passionate place.

You are about to encounter a most unusual "log book" entered by a most unusual sailing companion, Jim Kelly. This is an account of our overnight cruise onto—and into—Muscongus Bay, Maine, aboard a 26-foot sailing sloop.

But it is much more than that.

The patron saint of the education profession, John Dewey, once observed "We learn from experience…if we reflect upon our experience." Here, an accomplished, confident, seasoned school leader overcomes limited sailing experience, some physical impediments, and some well-founded apprehensions and jumps with both feet into an adventure. Reflecting on this experience, he gleans timeless nuggets of wisdom for himself and for the rest of us who would venture aboard a boat and into a schoolhouse.

I believe you will be moved, as I have been, by Jim's courage in undertaking this passage into unfamiliar waters with an unfamiliar captain. As many would attest, "sailing with Roland" is not always a day at the beach! And I think you'll be inspired by his persistence in surmounting heavy seas and a light stomach, by his growing skill in commanding the vessel, and by his abundant acumen and humor in finding a larger meaning in all of it.

So, dear reader, you are about to embark on a remarkable little cruise. Enjoy it. I've enjoyed it twice!

Roland S. Barth

Acknowledgments

I want to thank all of those educators with whom I have worked over the years, who have celebrated my successes and forgiven my transgressions. We learn by our mistakes and over the years, I have learned plenty.

I also wish to thank Rose Cooke, for her expertise and guidance in matters of style and grammar. Her advice was on target, the remaining errors of judgment are mine alone.

Last, and certainly not least, I wish again to thank Roland Barth, who showed me, by word and example, the value of taking a risk.

Preface

There are many lessons to be learned at sea, especially for a novice like me. As someone who is challenged by mobility issues brought on by a spinal cord injury, not to mention a propensity to become seasick, you may question my judgment to board a 26-foot sailboat that tends to rock with the swells of the ocean and the vicissitudes of the wind. And you would be right. But this was no ordinary journey. I entered the challenging realm of the rugged New England sailor with a far different motivation than most who venture onto the sea, enabling me to conquer my fears and learn some important lessons along the way.

I was a fortunate school principal to receive a grant that would allow me to meet one of my professional heroes. Roland Barth is an international author and lecturer. He is Harvard and Princeton educated, a former teacher, principal, and member of the Harvard faculty, where he started the Harvard Principal's Center. He has written numerous books and articles about the profession of education, and his book **Improving Schools From Within** has been my bible for the way schools should be run. He is also an avid sailor, dividing his time between Maine and Florida. I wanted to reach out to this icon and spend some quality time with him to discuss all matters related to our chosen field of education—in fact, I wanted to pick his brain. The Geraldine Dodge Foundation also thought this was a good idea, and funded my adventure. Fortunately, Roland was intrigued and extended an invitation for me to join him on his 26-foot Contessa sloop, the *Mare's Tail,* and sail the Muscongus Bay on an overnight expedition. I couldn't wait.

On an agreed upon day in August of 2006, I flew to Portland, rented a car, and drove the rest of the way to our rendezvous in Round Harbor, Maine. Arriving at the dock, I found Roland and his boat already waiting. With a hearty "welcome aboard" from the captain, I swallowed my fears, gathered what little courage I could muster, and stepped into an unfamiliar world. Despite his prodigious professional and nautical background, Roland's willingness to accept me into this world, coupled with his natural New England ability to make one feel comfortable instantly, helped me begin a highly personal and memorable experience.

Our journey started with the both of us getting wet!

Roland Barth in the Muscongus Bay.

CHAPTER 1: GETTING MY FEET WET

Before pulling up anchor and sailing out of the harbor, Roland asked if we could begin with a swim. It was his ritual for kicking off a good voyage. Who was I to refuse? After all, I was an invited guest. Invited guests don't refuse to partake in the rituals of those who invited them. Besides, it was hot as heck and jumping in the cool waters of Maine sounded like a good idea. Roland entered the water first, and in good form. As a physically challenged person, I had a bit more trouble with my entry. You see, I walk with a cane due to a spinal cord injury sustained decades ago, so it was more than a little difficult to stand on the side of the boat and jump in with any sense of grace or style. I managed, however, and the chilled Maine water brought instant life to a body tired from the long voyage up to Maine. Once in, we took an enjoyable swim around the boat and then decided it was time to cast off. Roland scurried up the ladder and into the boat like a squirrel fleeing up a tree. As I watched him go, it hit me like the bracing cold water upon entry that I was about to face my first big challenge of the trip—getting back into the boat. The rope and wood slat ladder attached to the boat for such a purpose were so slippery that I simply could not get a hold. Repeated attempts only resulted in a cramped foot and mounting frustration. We both examined the situation (Roland from the deck and me with my head just above water) not quite sure how we were going to get me back on board. Finally, Roland proposed rowing me to shore as I hung onto the rowboat, where I could stand up and get into the boat. He would then row us back to *Mare's Tail*. As we returned, Roland complimented me on my willingness to take such a risk despite some pretty difficult physical issues to overcome, and I learned my first lesson before leaving the harbor:

New Cruising Rule #1: Always begin each expedition with a swim, but make sure you can get back into the boat first.

As the principal of a grades 4/5 intermediate school with 570 plus students in a high performing, upper income, suburban community in New Jersey, I was not without daily challenges. Nor are you, I trust, no matter where you work. Pressures often come from the federal government (No Child Left Behind, Race to the Top, or some other platitude), the state department of education (high stakes testing and performance assessment), the central office, the teaching staff, the kids, and, of course, their parents. All are key stakeholders with very different perspectives in this enterprise we call education. These ever mounting difficulties are enough, at times, to lead you to the conclusion that it is best to keep your head down and just tow the line, to blindly follow whatever is dictated or mandated, and simply not rock the boat. It is certainly much easier to follow the path of least resistance. But then, what fun is that? Yes, I said fun. I would often say to my staff, "We have the best job in the country and if we're not having fun, we're not doing it right." Sometimes we need to buck the flow and work our way around the continuously growing bureaucracy that threatens to strangle us all. Sometimes we need to shift our focus from what needs to get done to what should be done. Sometimes we need to go headlong into something simply because it's the right thing to do, not the convenient thing to do. You can't help but feel better because of it, which leads me to my first new working rule:

New Working Rule #1: Jumping into anything with both feet is not without risk, but it can be extremely liberating.

Jim Kelly, the author, at the wheel.

CHAPTER 2: ANCHORS AWEIGH,
or is that *Away?*

When Roland and I got back into the boat, we hauled up the anchor and eased out of the harbor. I must admit that with the winds good and the water calm, it was exhilarating to be on the boat. Once clear of the harbor, we really began to move. However, any thoughts of this being a mini-vacation whereby I would sit comfortably in a lounge of some sort, sipping umbrella-decorated drinks, while someone else (Roland) manned the boat, were soon dispelled. Off and running, I received a "this is your show, so you take the helm" command from the captain, and quickly looked about so I could at least appear to know what he was talking about. The helm, fortunately for me, was not hard to miss, but what I was supposed to do with it remained a bit of a mystery. I had a rudimentary knowledge of how pushing it one way or the other determined direction, but how it tied into the sail, compass, and luff (new term for me-an indicator on the sail letting you know if you have the best direction into the wind to maximize sailing), I was soon to learn. Roland taught me how the weather can make it difficult to see where you are going in Maine, so it is a good idea to learn how to sail by the compass. It was such a beautiful day on the Bay that it was hard to imagine difficult weather. Still, I had been in Maine before and seen incredibly thick fog roll in to shore at a moment's notice, so I looked at the compass with renewed interest, leading me to my second new cruising rule:

New Cruising Rule #2: Always check the compass while your sailing, and don't forget to set your course.

In my career, I had the incredible good fortune to open a new school in a high performance district. I still remember the anxiety of those early days. I was hired in January of that year, brought on board in April, and given the task of opening the school that coming September. My staff was to be assembled from four different schools in the district, then housing children in three K-4 elementary schools and a 5-8 middle school. All district fourth grade students and fifth grade students would now be in my building; a fact that pleased some folks in the community and distressed quite a few others. My recollection was that it was running at about a fifty percent approval rating at the time, and we hadn't even opened yet. My immediate challenges were to meet with:

  a) Three disparate PTO groups and assure them that their children would be well cared for in a school outside their neighborhood,
  b) The Board of Education and assure them that the curriculum would be challenging and fulfilling, and
  c) The then disjointed staff of this new enterprise and ensure them that we could and would bond together with a common goal.

This last job was not an easy task, as all teachers and staff came from differing school cultures. We met frequently throughout the spring after school and on a few Saturdays. We talked, brainstormed, and discussed a myriad of issues, both critical and mundane. During those discussions, one thing became clearly evident: we all cared deeply about kids. We worked very hard to convey that fact to all members of our constituency, and eventually erected a banner that graced the school entry: *"Whenever you enter this building, you are loved first and taught second."*

That, in turn, leads me to my second new working rule:

New Working Rule #2: If you don't know where you're going, you'll never get there.

Jim Kelly, author, negotiating a path through boats and buoys.

CHAPTER 3: PUSHING AND PULLING

Although some people make it look easy (O' Captain, My Captain), there is a lot going on when you pilot a sailboat across a large body of water. Several different tasks have an impact on speed and direction, all of which you need to pay heed. Your boat, not to mention your crew or passengers, would be ill served if you focused on one at the expense of the others. Keeping an eye on the compass, especially in bad weather is a must, but does you no good if you don't also glance at the luff and keep your hand on the tiller to take advantage of the prevailing wind. That's a lot to take in for a landlubber like myself. It would have been much easier to feign ignorance (actually it would not have taken a great deal of feigning), or to suggest that I just wasn't up to it and could, therefore, only perform one of the lesser, but necessary, duties at hand. Though easier, it would not have provided me with the experience I both sought and received. My tasks—handling the tiller in such a way as to ride the very edge of the wind, while keeping the luff horizontal, and maintaining my course with an eye on the compass—put me in a whole new place mentally and led me to my third new cruising rule:

New Cruising Rule #3: With a firm hand on the tiller during a strong wind, it's easy to get "in the zone."

It is easy to get sidetracked in a job that is as diverse and challenging as educational administration. There are so many "have you got a minute?" distractions that come our way each day, you can almost empathize with the *insular principal* who surrounds his office with a gauntlet of desks and personnel to avoid actually meeting people. Almost. If we are to improve the preparation of future administrators, one key ingredient to the recipe for success needs to focus on the opportunities to experience interactive leadership in the field. There are precious few occasions for teachers to gain familiarity with what it means to lead under a variety of challenging conditions. This situation needs to change systemically; especially if we hope that new leaders emerge with the characteristics research indicates are important: a sense of shared responsibility and collegiality, an ability to work with management councils, compassion, and an open mind. It is not contradictory to suggest that it takes a great deal of effort to concentrate on knowing when to push and when to pull, when to suggest and when to firmly lay out a case, when to assist and when to provide much needed direction. None of this is for the timid, and it does lead me to my next new working rule:

New Working Rule #3: If you want to lead, then lead.

Reminders of it being busy out here.

CHAPTER 4: : WAKE UP CALL

As we sailed across the bay, there were an incredible number of buoys with a variety of colors strewn about, dotting the seascape like, as one youngster reported to Roland, "sprinkles on ice cream." Lobster boats pierced the quiet with their foghorns and loud motors, as they quickly went about their business. The buoys originally posed a bit of a challenge for me, because we had a rowboat in tow and it would be bad form to entangle our rowboat with the line attached to the buoy. Lobstermen take a dim view of that. The job, then, was to keep the buoys on my port side while keeping an eye on the sail and compass. It became less of an issue as my skills in sailing the boat improved, but the combination of so many buoys and noisy lobster boats were a constant reminder that people made a living out there, and that there were things they needed to do, in order to be successful. As I observed them ply their trade, it became clear how difficult their job really is, which led me to my next new cruising rule:

New Cruising Rule #4: The pots need checking early and often.

In my final job before retirement , I was the school's principal for twelve years. Before that, I spent four years as an administrator in another district, after nineteen years in the classroom in yet another. That's a long stretch by anyone's count, and if you're doing the math, I served in the field of education for thirty-five years, sixteen of them in educational administration. As an administrator, I alternately presided over a huge increase in enrollment, the hiring of new staff, the implementation of three new curriculum overhauls, and four new construction projects to accommodate the ever-growing number of students and staff. Clearly, it was vital to stay organized and on task. Each month brought not only new and exciting challenges, but also the normal operations of Back to School Night, concerts, conferences, trips, and pageants. Those are all important and necessary things that make school, well, school. They contribute to the social, emotional, and academic experience of all of the children who have a right to expect such things. It would be wrong, however, to look at our job as simply the opportunity to open the *November file* and see what major events would occupy our time and attention for that month. Events that would serve as an excuse to keep us from making personal contact. All too often, events that are predictable will emphasize a rote approach to our job, and encourage the insulation of the school's leader. Files are good for giving us a reminder, and to help organize our thoughts, but they should not be an excuse for hiding in our office. If we give in to that, we lose sight of what is truly important, interacting with the teachers and students who occupy the building and give it life. By leaving the file behind and spending more time in the halls and classrooms, we focus on new working rule #4:

New Working Rule #4: Tend to your workplace garden daily, and don't resort to the "make a file" system of management.

The wind at your sails.

CHAPTER 5: THE FORCE IS NOT ALWAYS WITH YOU

The weather was great, the wind strong, and I fooled myself into thinking I was really getting the hang of this sailing thing. You want me to bear right (sorry, starboard) and head towards that island? Okay, no problem. You want me to turn about in 100 feet? No sweat. I can do this, I told myself; yes, I can. However, I also, slowly began to understand what every good sailor knows instinctively: *you are not in control.* There are many things that dictate what you are going to do, and when you are going to do it. How high are the waves? How close are you getting to shore? Are there buoys in the way? And most importantly, you sail this boat *because* of the wind, not in spite of it. The wind will decide your speed, your direction, and the timing of your turns. The wind will even decide how much "fun" you are going to have. (Granted, that's a relative term). And the wind pretty well dictates new cruising rule five:

New Cruising Rule #5: You may have your hand on the tiller, but the wind tells you where to go.

How often in education have our opinions and actions been swayed by the winds of change—some of it good, some of it not so good? How often have you been taken by surprise at a PTA meeting, because an issue came up you didn't even know was an issue? How often have you brought what you thought was a great idea to a faculty meeting, only to be left asking, "What happened? Why didn't that idea fly?" Perhaps someone came up with an idea you hadn't considered. Or maybe others elaborated on your original idea and made it better. Or maybe no one liked your idea to begin with. The truth is we may always have on our hand on the tiller, but sometimes we are not in control of what direction the boat goes. It's the nature of the job, and the sooner we learn that important concept, the easier it will be to do our job well. We are not always "in control," and by that I mean we do not always have, or need to have, *the answer*. Instead, we need to encourage a healthy difference of opinion and, I daresay, give in to it, even at times when we may disagree strongly. If staff members feel they can weigh in on matters of importance, a strong, collaborative working atmosphere will grow. So, sometimes, even when reason tells you one thing, go where your gut tells you to go and embrace new working rule number five:

New Working Rule #5: Sometimes, you just need to go with the flow.

Avast and pay attention for it *is* a vast bay.

CHAPTER 6: LOOKING FOR RAND MCNALLY

There we were, cruising the Muscongus Bay on one of the most beautifully warm and clear summer days Maine could offer (there are two a year, I believe). I was getting a one on one sailing lesson from not only one of my all time favorite authors, but an expert sailor to boot. A good student, I paid heed to everything he told me. As well as I could, I learned how to read the compass and look at the luff to gauge my direction and whether or not I was maximizing the wind. When the wind died down a bit, Roland would take out a nautical chart and pore over it, as if seeing it for the first time. He explained our route to me with as much excitement as if we were crossing the Atlantic in a raft. And just when I thought looking at this chart was as clear as reading a Rand McNally along Route 1, he, my captain, tells me that we do have to be careful because there are often rocks and islands that appear and disappear with the tide. At that moment, I felt as if I had swallowed my tongue. What do you mean they disappear? You mean we can't see them? Are you serious? I don't give in to panic easily, but I must admit, I began looking around frantically for rapidly disappearing rock islands. And just when my imagination began to nurture a little doubt in my captain (no, he was not Bligh to my Mr. Christian, but let's face it— disappearing islands?), I stuttered the obvious question: "Do you know where they might be even when they disappear?" Without hesitation, and with a bit of a wry smile, he quoted a salty old New Englander, which instantly became new cruising rule six:

New Cruising Rule #6: "I don't know where they are; I just know where they ain't."

Our business of Education can often be compared to dancing through a minefield. And nothing says minefield like school construction. I've been through four such projects in my career, but I assure you that going through it once is enough penance for any bad deed you may have committed in your life. Each day brings with it the peaks and valleys normally associated with the unknown. Will they be delivering cement today? Will they be drilling just outside a classroom window to enhance the educational experience of those within? Will the workers be smoking or using language not appropriate for the ears of fourth graders? Will they decide to fire up the burner and do some hot tar roofing today without telling you first, which causes you to go into panic mode instantly, because you have to move four classes to an alternative space you don't have? You never quite know, and that's the point. But whether it's school construction, a challenge to a class placement, parental dissatisfaction with the level or delivery of the curriculum, or disappointment in your seating policy for the cafeteria at lunchtime, the fact is, we are constantly faced with surprises that seem to come from another dimension. Working rule six aptly describes this aspect of our job, and provides a maxim to follow:

New Working Rule #6: Expect the unexpected; it's always there, just below the surface.

Roland at the bow.

CHAPTER 7: ACHIEVING A STATE OF ZEN

I had been to Maine decades ago when I still had the ability and inclination to camp and hike. It was a wonderful experience and I remember it fondly. My wife and I drove up the coast to Acadia National Park, which is a beautiful area, loaded with what you might call typical Maine scenery: hills to climb, rocky coastline, fog laden harbors, cool air, cooler nights, and lobster, lobster, lobster. I thought I had enjoyed the quintessential Maine experience, and to a degree, I had. My voyage with Roland, however, was a real eye opener. Except for certain times of the day, which were active with lobster boats, it was largely quiet on the Muscongus Bay. It was sunny, you could see for miles, and the view from the water was breathtaking. Maine is just one of those places you have to see from a boat. Leaving and entering the harbor, viewing the coast as it moves on by, and seeing the greens, browns, and blooming flora with the sound of seagulls in your ear and cool salty air in your face, all makes for a spiritual moment. And no matter how serious the mission of this voyage, cruising rule seven became crystal clear:

New Cruising Rule #7: Take time out and enjoy the view.

I know some people, we all do, who are always looking over the next hill for meaning and fulfillment. The present moment, it seems, is never good enough, and cannot provide the excitement, the success, or the rewards they crave. This can also be true with some of the parents of the children we serve. We sometimes come across a few parents who are planning for a specific college for their child, while their child is in the first grade. I suppose it's the culture we find ourselves in. We never seem to be satisfied with what we have or how it works. We buy a computer with everything we could possibly need, and six months later the latest and greatest has even more, giving us, and our children, computer envy. Planning to start a regimen of exercise is derailed by thoughts of those new sneakers and workout gear that would help us get into it and do it right. You've probably heard it at work. If we only had __ we could __. Just fill in the blanks. While this dilemma isn't new, I do believe it is a pervasive and ongoing concern for the workplace. As you work with your staff in meeting the needs of the children in your care, you need to be conscious of this ever-growing phenomenon and do what you can to counter balance it by making each day a special one on a long and exciting journey. Trying to convince everyone that it's all about the trip and not necessarily the destination will be an uphill fight. In fact, a mission statement for us all could be new working rule seven:

New Working Rule #7: There is no better place to be than where you are, and no better time than now to make a difference.

Jim Kelly, author, slicing the Bay and gliding nearly upright.

CHAPTER 8: BEND IT LIKE BECKHAM

Sailing exposed me to a completely new vocabulary. While I may have heard of certain words, I wasn't quite sure how they applied to this new setting. Take "tack," for example. I had a vague idea of what it meant (like getting from point A to point B), but it always hung out there on the periphery of knowledge; something you hear, squirrel away somewhere, and nod knowingly about when you hear it again, never being quite sure, though, of its exact meaning. I found out quickly enough. Two words immediately came to mind while tacking: zig and zag. When looking out in the distance, it was quite easy for my captain to suggest that I should "head for that corner of the island" or "head for that clump of trees out on that piece of land," but quite another matter to do it. The wind (remember?) dictated where I actually went, and the designated location became something more of a suggestion, suggesting, if you will, new cruising rule eight:

New Cruising Rule #8: It's easier to draw a straight line than to follow one.

Mission statements, goals, and objectives tend to point the way for us. On some level, they are desired and necessary. Whether you're opening a new school, consolidating districts, or just starting a new school year, a collective rally around a philosophical flagpole can be refreshing, even galvanizing to all constituents. Even the federal catchphrase of "No Child Left Behind" is not without merit. Who can argue that sentiment? Yet that particular program very aptly points out that while such sentiments can and should serve as a guiding light for us all, much as a lighthouse for boats caught in a thick fog, there are always seen and unseen hazards to negotiate on the way to harbor. Confronting those challenges and interpreting the philosophical foundations creatively, without the constraints of bureaucratic overlay and threats of punishment, makes for a much richer environment for teachers, kids, and their parents. Keeping the educational system afloat through encouraged "out of the box" thinking allows for new working place rule 8:

New Working Rule #8: Flexibility prevents breakage.

Slowing it down a bit.

CHAPTER 9: BRIEF AND TO THE POINT

At one point, the wind died down somewhat, and this became great cause for concern. The joviality that characterized our journey thus far seemed to ebb with the wind flow. My captain, not happy at all with the sudden lack of sail power, decided to unfurl the jib (a small sail in the front of the boat) to help move us in a particular direction. I assisted as best I could—I stayed out of his way. Within seconds, the entire boat turned exactly in the direction he wished it to go. Within seconds, he accomplished this small but important objective with little effort on his part. As far as he was concerned, he used the very mild, but still available, wind and a small sail to do exactly what needed to be done, highlighting for me new cruising rule 9:

New Cruising Rule #9: It doesn't take much of the jib to turn your boat around.

The One Minute Manager by Ken Blanchard, Ph.D., published in the early 1980's, outlines how any manager can maximize his staff's effectiveness in a very short time. He believed that by applying his principles of identifying one minute goals, as well as giving one minute praises and one minute reprimands, a manager will accomplish more than by spending hours doing the same. In my role as principal, I often found it a real challenge to spend extensive amounts of time on anything. In place of lengthy formal meetings, I preferred to walk the building, taking every advantage to inquire about someone's family, compliment someone on what I noticed about their classroom, or remind someone of a deadline. I found that most teachers I'd see on my rounds would also ask if I "had a minute" to discuss an issue, which could be resolved in not much more time than that. Rather than look upon that as some kind of failure to devote enough time on task, I preferred to view it as new working rule 9:

New Working Rule #9: A "one minute manager" can accomplish great things in a short time.

Dead calm.

CHAPTER 10: RED FLAGS

Sailing can be a relative term; relative, of course to the amount of available wind. Sometimes, it simply isn't there. With the enjoyment factor high (given abundant sun, clear views, and smooth seas), I thought this wasn't too much to be concerned about. After all, here I was, sailing the coast of Maine discussing education with one of my personal heroes, a well known expert in the field, so what's not to like? Then the wind died. We sat there on water flat as a pancake, not going anywhere. What I didn't realize is that sailors take this as a personal affront. Sailors want to be sailing. It's why they have a sailboat. There are many challenges, both natural and otherwise, any good sailor is willing to face. Some would argue that they look for a challenge just to say they confronted and overcame it. The lack of available wind, believe me, is not one of them. And when the wind dies and it gets dead calm, and you come face to face with new cruising rule 10:

New Cruising Rule #10: Sometimes you just have to use a motor.

A teacher is often described as being a jack-of-all-trades. All teachers tend to the myriad of challenges that fall under the social, emotional, and educational needs of the many children in their care. They are relied upon for budget preparation, trip planning, curriculum implementation, and values education. It's no wonder many new teachers burn out before they have ample opportunity to light up the profession. No one likes being in the position of not knowing something, least of all teachers, who are often targeted as a societal scapegoat by the very society they serve. No one wants to give even the appearance of failure. When I was a teacher in the classroom, I tried a great many new things: new strategies to deliver instruction, new activities to make it exciting, and some experimentation on how to assess what it was I wanted my students to learn. I was blessed to have a principal who valued such experimentation—someone who knew that teaching, not an exact science, would only benefit from the scientific process of testing hypotheses. In this era of *high stakes testing*, we have a teaching force reluctant to try anything new: people who are hesitant to tinker with and stretch creative ideas, a work force frightened to stick their neck out. I would contend that if we are to succeed as an institution, indeed as a society, we need to afford teachers the *opportunity* of failure. By doing so, we recognize that we learn by failing , and that by learning in such a way, we all move forward. We need to make a conscious effort to create a working environment where risk is not a four-letter word. We need to allow new working rule 10 to become the order of the day:

New Working Rule #10: It's okay to take a risk, and to ask for and get help.

Beauty comes easy along the coast of Maine.

CHAPTER 11: I'LL HUFF AND I'LL PUFF

When we decided to anchor for the evening, it was not without good cause. Sailing is hard work; you get tired in the great outdoors pulling and pushing the tiller against a strong wind. It also made sense to get set up for the night before the mosquitoes paid us a visit. So, it was with a personal sense of relief that we pulled into a quiet harbor facing the sea, giving us a chance to view a beautiful sunset on a dead flat body of water. Other, yacht size boats, tall and majestic, were already anchored and not far off, sitting there like two large beautiful swans on a lake. The peace and serenity was palpable. Later that night, as I drifted off to sleep with the soft lapping of water against the hull, I contentedly thought, "I can do this, and you know what, it's not so bad." At 2:00 am, I changed my mind. The boat was doing some serious rocking, like one of those rides I no longer dared go on at the Jersey shore. The halyard was rapidly slapping against the mast it was tied to, keeping time with my new mantra, "I won't throw up, I won't throw up." My captain awoke with a start, declaring that the wind had shifted and was now coming from the north. He then did what any good sailor would do at a time like this—he promptly went back to sleep. Well, I didn't throw up, but I didn't sleep much either. And at the crack of dawn, when the winds died down again and calm was blessedly restored by Mother Nature, I crept out to the back deck looking very much the worse for wear. When Roland joined me, he noted my condition and saw me staring at the empty spot where I believed our neighbors had anchored the night before. "Well", I confidently said, "looks like they up anchored and went for safety some time last night." Without missing a beat, he told me to turn around and there, in plain sight were the two boats I thought had left, outlining quite clearly new cruising rule 11:

New Cruising Rule #11: A strong north wind in the middle of the night can turn your world around.

When I was a neophyte teacher back in the day, the culture of schools was very different. Teachers were pretty much in charge of what went on in their classrooms, administrators were pretty much in charge of running their schools, and parents often cared enough to give the following advice: "If he gets out of hand, you have my permission to hit him." Some of that needed to change, of course; corporal punishment never was a strategy I practiced or condoned. And the sort of loose, free-form cultural milieu that existed at the time, worked only if those who worked within it promoted collegiality, risk taking, group goal setting, and the creative delivery of instruction. Not always the case then or now, unfortunately, as evidenced by the changes demanded by A Nation At Risk and No Child Left Behind. Our national government certainly has, and should have, a vested interest in paying a great deal more attention to the institution of education than it has in the past, as it bears directly on the economic, political, and social health of our country. Unfortunately, some of that attention can be politically motivated, assigning blame instead of offering much needed appropriate assistance. I don't think it too bold to say that sometimes our government even appears to go so far as to advocate for the very destruction of our system of education, which I happen to believe is the backbone of our democracy. Teaching is no longer an isolated and lonely profession to be left alone and evolve as it will. Today, no matter where you work, each and every time you step into a classroom, you have parental expectations, budget considerations, high stakes testing, and governmental legislation right in there with you, pointing out for us all the need for new working rule 11:

New Working Rule #11: Pay *very* close attention to the external factors that influence what we do.

Casting off for dinner.

CHAPTER 12: LOOKING FOR LOBSTER IN ALL THE WRONG PLACES

Prior to bedding down for the evening, there was the little matter of dinner. It was my fervent hope that somewhere in the hold, there was a cooked lobster with my name on it. I could almost taste it as I pictured it in my mind: red, juicy, delicious, and swimming in butter. Can there be anything else on the mind of a hungry out-of-state visitor? What do you think of if not lobster when you are traveling anywhere in Maine? As far as I was concerned, the conversation I encountered throughout the day was excellent, right on target and to the point, but it could only improve while dining on this quintessential Maine repast. After all, I was with a native of the state, and it was a logical assumption that the boat was loaded with these native crustaceans. Instead, I was handed a fishing rod and reel! With hearty good cheer I was told we were actually going to fish for dinner. I hid my admittedly touristy dismay and, after a brief lesson, began to cast out. After what seemed like a reasonable time, I reeled in my line looking in vain for the seemingly elusive mackerel we so earnestly sought. I cast out and reeled in again...and again, and again, and again. Still nothing. It quickly became clear that I was not much of a fisherman, but I can tell you in all honesty that hunger is a great motivator. While ultimately I was not very successful, new cruising rule 12 came into play:

New Cruising Rule # 12: When fishing for your dinner, everyone gets religion.

A woman I used to work with—her name was Alice Ruffer—died of cancer. She was there at the creation of our school, and was a big part of its soul. She had been selected along with others in the district to open that institution because she was a good teacher. She was a good teacher not because she could put together a good lesson plan and effectively deliver it, although she sure could. She was a good teacher because of who she was. She had a smile that went from one ear to the other and back again. When accompanied by her full and spontaneous laugh, she lit up a room. She liked simple things, like arts and crafts, and really enjoyed watching Martha Stewart make something useful and attractive out of everyday objects. It was a metaphor for her life. You see, she truly loved children. She loved their rawness, their incompleteness, and the fact they were a constant work in progress. She had a special place in her heart, truth be told, for those who fell under the category of what my grandparents would call a hop in the keister: kids who did bad things but weren't really bad, more of a pest than anything. From her perspective, they just needed more love. Kids knew all of these things about her even though she never had to tell them. They knew instinctively that no matter what, she was on their side. She approached her job without fanfare, and did what had to be done with a passion. Her long-lasting legacy for me and for all who were blessed to know her is new working rule #12:

New Working Rule #12: A little bit of love, passion, and nurturing goes a very long way.

Roland agrees to an interview.

CHAPTER 13: REACH OUT AND TOUCH SOMEONE

Time passes slowly when you're on a boat. And let's face it, there is no TV, large screen or otherwise. The primary means of passing time, and the essential purpose of this voyage, was to engage in conversation. While I had a list of questions I wanted to ask Roland, much of our time was spent in an informal exchange of ideas, which was probably much more valuable. We covered a wide range of topics throughout the course of the day, but anytime you get two educators in a room, or on a boat, their craft always becomes the dominant topic of discussion. Being cornered on a boat like we were could have been a dangerous and difficult situation. I could have been an obnoxious and challenging wordsmith paparazzi, looking to poke holes in anything Roland has ever written or said. He could have pontificated on a good many aspects of our chosen profession, and with good reason, causing me to speak little and think less. Fortunately, it was not in the nature of either one of us to behave in such a way. Our conversations were free flowing, with respect and careful consideration to speaker and listener on both ends. This clearly indicated what passed for new cruising rule #13:

New Cruising Rule #13: When at sea, no matter how long, choose good company.

I always ate lunch in the faculty room. Besides satisfying a basic biological need, it gave me a great opportunity to connect with the most important people in our school. It was always important to me to make a daily connection with the teachers in our building, even on matters that may seem trivial, and I hope it mattered to them. My comments, questions, praise, and perhaps even just my presence showed that I valued what they did and who they were. I was available to them, allowing me, sometimes, to put out a fire, quell a rumor, clarify my position, or just tell a joke to lift their spirits on a challenging day. Reaching out to my colleagues emphasizes my core belief about educational administration. It's not really about the policies we create and it's not about the procedures we put in place. And it's not about the paperwork or programs that consume so much of our time. It's about the people. The best administrator I ever worked with was my principal in my first teaching job. His name is Gene Hastings and he knew this well. He has always been my mentor and my friend, and while he is long retired now, the lesson he taught so many of us over the years, and which, sadly, does not exist in all places, is new working rule #13:

New Working Rule #13: Making daily personal connections breeds a cohesive, dedicated staff, and is the most important thing you can do.

The road home is swift with a strong wind at your back.

CHAPTER 14: IN PRAISE OF AN IRISH PRAYER

On the morning after the night of no sleep, it took me quite a while to get it together and appear somewhat normal. I stress the word *somewhat*. No, I *stretch* the word somewhat, as I was tired, dizzy, and not too sure on my feet. Not so my captain. He awoke with the positive energy of someone who had a good night's rest, as good sailor's can, despite foul weather. We conducted a more formal interview over questions I composed before the journey and sat down to a hearty breakfast of cereal accompanied by hand picked Maine blueberries from his very own garden. Despite his natural good nature and ability to make me feel as comfortable as I possibly could, the previous night's disruption to my biorhythm left me a bit distressed. We listened to the marine weather forecast indicating thunder and lightning storms for late afternoon and early evening, accompanied by high swells. My head turned as swiftly on my neck as that famous scene from the movie *The Exorcist*, and I said, without hesitation, "Roland, please don't take this personally, but I can't spend another night on this boat." We both agreed on another full morning of sailing, which was outstanding by the way, before heading for port. After that particular forecast, heading for port around lunchtime made me feel that *there's no place like home* and think of new cruising rule #14:

New Cruising Rule #14: At the end of an arduous journey, it's good to have a strong wind at your back.

After a long run, I reached the pinnacle of my career in education, culminating in receiving the 2007 New Jersey Principal's and Supervisor's Association Principal of the Year award for Visionary Leadership, followed by my retirement in July of that same year. I have been able to serve in the education business for 35 years, and I count each one as a step along a fantastic and wonderful journey. I have learned many important lessons, some of them the hard way, but all of them valuable. Perhaps the most important is a point I have made in a variety of ways throughout this story. It is a recurring theme in every rule listed, in every lesson I learned, and in every discussion that took place on this voyage. It is working place rule #14 and it is, I believe, the beginning and end point for an effective educational administrator or any manager of people:

New Working Rule #14: Ultimately, we are as successful as the level of support we engender among our staff.

The ultimate goal for us both.

CHAPTER 15: GOOD ENDINGS
When we sailed into port, the sun was still high and the winds favorable, making for an outstanding approach to the finish line. Due to the fatigue of holding the boat against a strong wind as well as a lack of sleep, I was quite exhausted. Roland was instantly concerned that the tide wasn't high enough to get me to the dock to unload. We may, he said, "have to wait a couple of hours" before depositing my tired body on dry land. "Nothing doing," I said. I told him if he got me to the dock, he and I would enjoy lobster for lunch at the pound on top of the hill (I *would* have my lobster before leaving Maine). We were there in seconds (even an icon gets hungry) and with feet planted firmly, once again, on terra firma, we made our wobbly way (at least on my part) to a well-deserved lunch for us both. As we discussed the trip and what I learned from it, I couldn't help thinking that this pillar of education was that and a great deal more; just as all that he taught me about sailing was that and a great deal more. And while this isn't a cruising or working rule, I will close by sharing my final observation:

To end your journey by sharing oysters, lobsters, and an ice-cold beer with a newfound friend is not a bad thing at all.

NEW CRUISING RULES FOR THIS VOYAGE

New Cruising Rule #1: Always begin each expedition with a swim, but make sure you can get back into the boat first.

New Cruising Rule #2: Always check the compass while you're sailing, and don't forget to set your course.

New Cruising Rule #3: With a firm hand on the tiller during a strong wind, it's easy to get "in the zone."

New Cruising Rule #4: The pots need checking early and often.

New Cruising Rule #5: You may have your hand on the tiller, but the wind tells you where to go.

New Cruising Rule #6: "I don't know where they are, I just know where they ain't."

New Cruising Rule #7: Take time out and enjoy the view.

New Cruising Rule #8: It's easier to draw a straight line than to follow one.

New Cruising Rule #9: It doesn't take much of the jib to turn your boat around.

New Cruising Rule #10: Sometimes you just have to use a motor.

New Cruising Rule #11: A strong north wind in the middle of the night can turn your world around.

New Cruising Rule #12: When fishing for your dinner, everyone gets religion.

New Cruising Rule #13: When at sea, no matter how long, choose good company.

New Cruising Rule #14: At the end of an arduous journey, it's good to have the wind at your back.

NEW WORKING RULES FOR THIS VOYAGE

New Working Rule #1: Jumping into anything with both feet is not without risk, but it can be extremely liberating.

New Working Rule #2: If you don't know where you're going, you'll never get there.

New Working Rule #3: If you want to lead, then lead.

New Working Rule #4: Tend to your workplace garden daily, and don't resort to the "make a file" system of management.

New Working Rule #5: Sometimes, you just need to go with the flow.

New Working Rule #6: Expect the unexpected; it's always there, just below the surface.

New Working Rule #7: There is no better place to be than where you are, and no better time than now to make a difference.

New Working Rule #8: Flexibility prevents breakage.

New Working Rule #9: A "one minute manager" can accomplish great things in a short time.

New Working Rule #10: It's okay to take a risk, and to ask for and get help.

New Working Rule #11: Pay *very* close attention to the external factors that influence what we do.

New Working Rule #12: A little bit of love, passion, and nurturing goes a very long way.

New Working Rule #13: Making daily personal connections breeds a cohesive, dedicated staff, and is the most important thing you can do.

New Working Rule #14: Ultimately, we are as successful as the level of support we engender among our staff.

Bibliography

Barth, Roland S. (2003). <u>Lessons Learned</u>, Thousand Oaks, CA: Corwin Press.

Barth, Roland S. (1990). <u>Improving Schools From Within</u>, San Francisco, CA: Jossey-Bass, Inc.

Barth, Roland S. (1980). <u>Run School Run</u>, Cambridge MA: Harvard University Press.

Bennis, Warren (1997). <u>Managing People is Like Herding Cats</u>, Provo, Utah: Executive Excellence Press.

Covey, Stephen R. (1991). <u>Principle-Centered Leadership</u>, New York NY: Fireside.

Sergiovanni, Thomas (1992). <u>Moral Leadership</u>, San Francisco, CA: Jossey-Bass, Inc.

ABOUT THE AUTHOR

Jim Kelly has been a middle school teacher, a vice-principal, a principal, a Co-Director of the New Jersey State History Fair, a consultant for the New Jersey Foundation for Educational Administration, a current Board member of the Global Learning Project, a non-profit, and Past-President of the Morris County Association of Elementary and Middle School Administrators. He has been the recipient of numerous education awards such as the *New Jersey Governor's Teacher Award*, two *Geraldine Dodge Foundation Grants*, and by acclamation of his school staff, received the *New Jersey Principal's and Supervisor's Association Principal of the Year Award for Visionary Leadership in 2007.* Jim has authored two professional books: **Student-Centered Teaching for Increased Participation** and **In Search of Leadership**.

The Lost Treasure , available on Amazon.com, is Jim's first novel. His love of mysteries, adventures, and everything about Sherlock Holmes, helped in the creation of eleven-year-old Bobby Holmes and his cousin Brenda Watson. **Tommy Ails: Good For What Ails You**, a soon to be released novel for adults, is a humorous off-beat mystery.

Jim currently lives in New Jersey and Sarasota, Florida, with his wife Bronwen. They have three children, Peter, Alex, and Brianna.

Email: jmkellyauthor@gmail.com

Made in the USA
Middletown, DE
16 February 2021